Toddler Discipline:

Proven Toddler Discipline Strategies for Stress & Guilt-Free Parenting

Marie C. Foster

inaccuracies.

Table of Contents

Introduction:

One of the biggest struggles that parents face is knowing how to discipline their toddlers. If you have ever heard of the 'terrible twos', then you may have an inkling of how difficult it can be—for more reason than one.

During the toddler years, your baby starts to define their place in the world. They are going to challenge your authority, push boundaries, and throw fits when the world does not move according to how they think it should.

The second reason that the toddler years are so difficult is because of the barrage of information that parents must sort through. Your child's doctor, friends and other parents, your parents and in-laws, and all sorts of people will think that they know the best way to raise your child. Through all this input that they offer, you must decide what is valuable and what just doesn't fit within your parenting style.

The other problem comes when trying to find information on the Internet. Like in real life, information comes from various sources—and much of it is contradictory to other ideas you find.

Fortunately, by owning this book, you are taking the first step in finding some solid, accurate information about disciplining your toddler. The ideas in this book are written using a balance between scientific information and personal experience raising my boys, who are 2 and 4 currently.

With my first son, I had a lot of trial-and-error and, of course, the input of anyone that I talked to about my kids. I have created this book with a desire to educate parents about different discipline strategies that exist, so you don't have to dig for information and guess about what works and doesn't work. The strategies are proven effective, from my home to yours, and heavily based on scientific studies that have been done concerning toddler discipline. At the end of the book, there is also a chapter on disciplining special needs kids, which requires a slightly different technique than most toddlers.

This book is going to serve a great purpose in your life. It will help you develop discipline strategies that you can use without feeling guilty or stressed. It is not uncommon for parents to question their methods, especially if they feel they must yell or hit their child. The truth is, however, that you do not have to scream at your child or spank them to get their attention. By employing the strategies that follow in this book, you will learn how to properly discipline your child, so they grow into a well-rounded, emotionally healthy adult.

It is never too late to take the first step to proper toddler discipline. So, let's get started!

Chapter 1: Essentials to Effective Toddler Discipline

Chapter 1: Essentials to Effective Toddler Discipline

From the moment your child comes into the world, its eyes are on you. As he or she learns and grows, you will see yourself in the things that they do—like the way that your baby smiles or the chuckle they get when you tickle them. Unfortunately, as babies grow into toddlers, they become more defiant versions of themselves. They start to make their place in the world, test boundaries, and are prone to occasional fits of outrageous behavior, as they try to explore all that is around them. It's as your child leaves infancy and moves into these trying times that toddler discipline becomes necessary for healthy development of your little boy or girl.

One of the problems that parents sometimes face is finding a toddler discipline strategy that they can use without feeling guilty. For example, when you spank your child, it does not make you feel better following the punishment. For most parents, it makes them feel worse and question their abilities. Fortunately, by picking up this book, you have made the first commitment to stress-free and guilt-free parenting.

What is Toddler Discipline?

Toddler discipline has a profound effect on your child's future and mental health. While the word discipline can come across as harsh under certain contexts, this is caused by a misinterpretation of its meaning. Discipline should not always mean punishment. When it comes to toddler discipline, it means teaching and guidance, rather than punishing your toddler when they do not listen to you.

There will be times that you want to punish your toddler. This is because as your child learns from you, he or she is given the choice as to whether they listen or not. They will not always be obedient—and this warrants some kind of response. If you do not respond to their behaviors at all, they will continue to push boundaries and escalate.

Discipline Myths

There are many ways that you can discipline a toddler, however, not all methods are going to work. There are many myths regarding disciplining children, including:

- Yelling Louder Will Get My Toddler's Attention- It can be very easy to yell at a toddler, especially as they defiantly knock over their fourth drink that day or throw their toys through the house. The problem with yelling is that when it becomes normalized, it loses its effectiveness. Instead of hearing you because you are yelling louder, your child will learn to tune it out and go on with their bad behavior. This means when it is important, or they are doing something dangerous, you will not be able to get their attention.

- My Parents Spanked Me, and I Turned Out Okay- According to a study published in 2014, 65% of women and 76% of men supported spanking a misbehaving child. However, numerous studies have proven that spanking does little to achieve a toddler's behavior. Not only will it not change bad behavior in the long-term, it has shown positive correlations to antisocial tendencies, aggression, and poor mental health. Some studies even suggested that the long-term results of an occasional smack on the bottom had the same effect as child abuse.

- Negotiation Never Works-People who are concerned

with being overly permissive and ending up with a 'bad' kid will tell you that you should never negotiate with a child. However, that is simply not the truth. The key to negotiation is to let the child make a decision, but to keep the cards in your hand by giving them a few acceptable options and then letting them make a choice. We will explore this idea more in depth later in the book.

- You Should Never Say 'Yes'- Another common myth is that if you tell your child 'yes,' you are failing to give them the boundaries that they need to thrive. But, what if your toddler is asking for something reasonable? If you are worried about setting boundaries, follow the 'yes' with a condition. Then, explain the reason why before your toddler has a chance to ask. For example, "Yes, you can play with Play-Doh but only if you pick up your toys. Otherwise, we will not be able to see any Play-Doh that has fallen on the floor and needs picked up when you are done."

- Strict Parents Are Good Parents- It is hard not to judge when you see a toddler flailing on the floor of the supermarket, thinking that the parent needs to be stricter. The problem with this mindset is that when we are too strict with kids, we do not teach them empathy, compassion, and understanding. After all, they are looking to us as role models on how to treat other people.

- You Should Not Have to Repeat Yourself- The truth is that toddlers have a short attention span. While they will get the general message you are trying to send from day-to-day, you should expect to repeat yourself—a lot. Just like with learning counting, colors, shapes, and the alphabet, toddlers learn through repetition that helps form the connections in their mind. It can be frustrating when you feel like you are constantly repeating yourself, but it is necessary to communicate clearly with your toddler.

Do not worry if you have been guilty of any of these things in the past—it is never too late to take a new approach to discipline. In this book, you will learn many effective tactics for discipline, designed to give you a variety of methods for different situations you may encounter with your toddler. Through your own personal journey with toddler discipline, your parenting style, study, and research, you will be able to shape a disciplinary plan that words. Additionally, you will learn more about what you should expect from your toddler—including behavior and response to discipline.

As you read, keep in mind that raising any child (not just yours) comes with its challenges. They can cause stress, self-doubt, and worry over whether you are getting it right—but just take a deep breath. These days will be over before you know it and raising a child is always a rewarding experience in the end.

Why Toddler Discipline is Important

The key to toddler discipline is a balance. You cannot punish your child so much that they have psychological scars, which last long after childhood. However, you cannot be so permissive that your toddler does not learn boundaries. You must be strict, but you also must care enough that your toddler understands that the rules you set forth are for their best interest. Some of the benefits of good toddler discipline include:

- Prevents Physical Struggles- When you choose aggressive methods like spanking, it can cause the problem with your toddler to escalate. They also learn that this behavior is acceptable. By finding a better discipline problem, you can encourage your son or daughter to behave without physical violence.

- Better Management of Anxiety- When a toddler looks to you to set boundaries, they are testing you to reassure themselves. Your toddler does not want to be in charge. What they do want is to feel assured that you are in control of the situation. If a child does not have this, they can develop anxiety because they feel pressured to set adult boundaries and make adult situations.

- Proper Discipline Encourages Safety- The major goal of discipline should never be to punish—it should be to ensure your child's safety and health. Consequences must be given so that your toddler knows they cannot run out into the street without looking. They can also be used to promote health and prevent obesity.

For example, teaching your toddler to eat a wide range of healthy foods and saying 'no' to obsessive snacking habits.

- Better Management of Frustration, Anger, and Other Emotions- If you give in every time that your child has a temper tantrum, you are sending the message that he or she should continue to act this way to get what they want. When you discipline your child by ignoring mild tantrums, your toddler learns that society will not do what they want if they act in that manner. Time out also has a purpose following an angry outburst—by reinforcing the idea of taking time to reflect on the anger. Finally, using praise helps deal with frustration, especially when you credit your child with continuing to work hard at something, despite their frustration.

- Encourages Good Choices- When you discipline your toddler appropriately, you teach them how to make decisions. Healthy discipline can encourage them to consider alternative ways for getting needs met. Some of the skills that can be learned include self-regulation, impulse control, and problem solving. Rather than focusing on punishments, teach your child consequences. These are more effective in teaching them about their mistakes, making it less likely that they will choose poorly in the future.

Disciplining Your Toddler: What to Expect

Below, you will find some general tips for toddler discipline. Specific techniques will be discussed later in the book, but this is an overview of how you might apply these techniques to disciplining your child:

- Positive Reinforcement- Praise and positive reinforcement will go a long way in teaching your child to behave well. When you tell them they are doing something good, and your actions and tone of voice reflect this positivity, they will get good feelings from it. The positive way they are experiencing the activity will make it more likely they will repeat this good behavior in the future.

- Ignore the Bad (to an Extent)- When you child throws a temper tantrum, they are trying to get your attention. If you yell or respond, you are giving them what they want. Provided they are not harming themselves or someone else, let your toddler cry it out. This can be embarrassing if you are somewhere like the store, but if you give into what they want just to get them to be quiet, you are encouraging them to recreate the scenario in the future. If you cannot stand the temper tantrum, leave any groceries you have not paid for behind and walk out to the car. Let them sit inside with you until they can calm down or go home and try shopping another time.

- Logical Consequences- This form of discipline involves creating a consequence if your toddler behaves. For example, tell your child (do not yell) that if they do not pick up their toys, you will take them away for the day. Set a time limit or react if your child does not start moving to pick up the toys. Once they do not listen, follow through on the consequence immediately and ignore their protest/tantrum that may result.

- Natural Consequences- If your child is not doing something dangerous, one of the best things you can do is let the situation unfold naturally. The key is not coming to their rescue after the event, no matter how much they cry. For example, imagine that your toddler keeps throwing their cookies on the floor. Instead of yelling or punishing them, warn them that they will not have any cookies if they throw them all on the floor. Let this natural consequence unfold and do not give them any more cookies once they have run out.

- Redirection- When your child seems like they might make a fuss over what you have just told them not to do, re-direct them. For example, imagine that two siblings are fighting over a toy. You can give it to the child that had it first if you saw what happened. Otherwise, remove the toy and put it up. Redirect the siblings to a new activity, either one that they can do together or to two separate activities that they can work on alone.

- Time Out- It is not uncommon for parents to

protest the time out method, especially if their child is resistant. The problem in these cases is not usually the technique (time out) but the way that time out is enforced. Before your child has a chance to behave poorly, set rules with them about the types of behaviors (hitting, throwing toys, etc.) that will get them in time out. This should be limited to 2-3 things that your child should remember. Then, you will set a location and length of time for the time out. If the infraction happens, stick to the guidelines you set, regardless of your toddler's reaction. Another option is using one area for quiet time and another for time out, which is the more severe consequence. We will talk more deeply about this later.

- Withholding Privileges- When you withhold privileges, it must be done in a way that your toddler can form the connection between what is being taken away and the bad behavior. You can take away something valuable to your child, like a toy, television, or another privilege, but you should never take away something that is a necessity (like food). You should also do the punishment immediately since children under 6-7 years of age do not have the mental capacity to understand something like losing TV in the evening being connected to refusing to pick up their toys that morning.

CHAPTER SUMMARY:

1. Toddler discipline should not have the goal of punishing misbehavior, but teaching between right and wrong. Toddlers are at a point in their life when they are very

impressionable and the way that you choose to discipline them can affect them greatly later in life. There are many myths regarding discipline that you should take note of, including that yelling and spanking are effective. Do your research to learn about the scientific reasons that discipline may or may not work, rather than listening to the anecdotes of other people's advice.

2. Disciplining your toddler is about balance. You will need to set rules firmly, but you must also show compassion and understanding. When discipline is done correctly, toddlers grow into well-behaved, well-rounded children. Some of the benefits

include prevention of physical altercations, anxiety management, the safety of your toddler, emotional regulation, and encouragement of good choices.

3. There are many discipline strategies that will work in this book. What it boils down to is what is most effective for your child. Often, you will vary the discipline based on the bad behavior. Some of the techniques that will be discussed in this book include positive reinforcement, ignoring bad behavior, logical and natural consequences, redirecting, time out, and withholding things.

YOUR QUICK START ACTION STEP: EVALUATE DISCIPLINE MYTHS

Is there anything specific that you have heard regarding toddler discipline that you are skeptical about? Take twenty or thirty minutes to learn what you can about the most common discipline myths and take stock of which ones you may use in your parenting style. Do not worry if you find a few—no parent is perfect. By identifying these, you can start to understand which aspects of your toddler discipline practices that you may want to alter or replace.

Chapter 2: Understanding Toddler Behavior

Chapter 2: Understanding Toddler Behavior

If you are like me, or almost any other parent for that matter, there are times when your child's behavior just has you asking 'why?' The truth is that even though you see your toddler's behavior as strange or frustrating, it is most likely a normal reaction to the changes they are going through in life. Toddlers often act out for an underlying reason, often because they do not understand how to communicate their needs and what they are going through.

Why Your Toddler Doesn't Listen

The 'Terrible Twos' are most likely to happen between the ages of 2 and 3. During this time, toddlers are learning that they are individuals apart from their parents or other caregivers. They strike out as independent entities, which leads to their desire to assert themselves during this stage. Toddlers are also more likely to act independently and want to try things for themselves, as well as communicate what they like and do not like. This is the reason that most toddlers choose not to listen to what we tell them—they are trying to express themselves and set themselves apart from their parents. Even so, this can be problematic when we are trying to provide guidance and keep them safe. There are several reasons that your child may be acting out, including:

- They Don't Understand Their Feelings- The toddler age is when your child is emotionally mature enough to start experience emotions. This includes complex feelings like embarrassment, pride, guilt, frustration, joy excitement, jealousy, anger, and shame. Another problem is how quickly their mood changes—one moment your child can happily be licking a popsicle and the next they may be sobbing because some of it melted onto their hand.

- They Lack Self-Control- Another reason toddlers may act out is because they do not know to express how they are feeling. This means that when they are angry with someone, for example, they do not know how to say, "I am mad" or even relate what they are feeling with anger. Instead, they may lash out by throwing a tantrum, hitting, or screaming. As your child learns to identify these emotions and appropriately respond to them, they will start to make better behavioral choices.

- They are Over stimulated- Have you ever spent a day out in the sun and been exhausted at the end of it? This is from overstimulation from sunlight in your eyes and on your skin. Toddlers can experience sensory overload too, though they experience it with much less stimulation than adults. Sometimes, toddlers need time to themselves and to be away from it all. If you have ever had a long, exhausting day and then been short-tempered with your partner later, then you have experienced a similar feeling to this.

- They Have a Need that is Not Being Met- Toddlers are incredibly sensitive to all things during this time, not just their emotions. If your child is hungry, thirsty, or over-tired, chances are they are going to misbehave. Unfortunately, they cannot always identify these things and tell you what they need.
- They Want Attention- When toddlers are looking

for their parents to pay attention, they will go to any lengths to get it. Have you ever told your toddler that you were in the middle of something, only to find them getting in trouble not even five minutes later? Odds are, when you do not give them the attention they are seeking, they will misbehave to get negative attention instead. Either way, your focus is on them.

- They Are Having a Bad Day- One of the things that parents often forget is that they have bad days. Some days, you may feel 'off' or irritable for what seems like no reason. Toddlers can have this problem too. When we do not give them the same regard for their feelings that adults have, it does not empathy or compassion.

How Understanding Toddler Behavior Impacts Toddler Discipline

The emotional changes that a toddler goes through can be wild and unpredictable. This is the reason that toddlers often act out—they do not know how to handle the emotions inside them. When you consider toddler behavior, it is important to look at it with empathy. It is not a firm hand that is needed during these times—but an empathetic approach that teaches a toddler how to handle their experiences. You should be loving and guiding, rather than strict and distant.

Benefits of Creating a Toddler Discipline Strategy

Something to keep in mind as you read this book is that you will need to adjust the discipline strategy that you use based on your own child's habits and responses to your discipline. By observing how the different methods work with your child, you will be able to come up with a toddler discipline strategy. The benefits of developing this include:

- Consistency- When you are consistent with what you expect of your toddler, and the resulting disciplinary action, you send a strong, clear message. Your toddler starts to associate certain behaviors with the discipline that results. Additionally, they learn what behaviors make you pleased with them.
- Clear Expectations- The consistency that is created with a well-thought-out strategy gives your toddler clear expectations to live up to. They know what

they can and cannot do and learn the difference between wrong and write. This is advantageous because it will encourage better decision making and behavior from your toddler in the future.

- Self-Control- When you create a strategy for toddler discipline, it helps your toddler learn what behaviors are and are not acceptable. As you help them learn to label and manage the emotions they are feeling, it promotes better self-control and good mental health.
- Decision-Making- Something that we must

do as parents is teach our children how to thrive later in life. We will not always be there to make decision for them, nor should we be. As your toddler shows their individuality and their capability for making decisions, it is important to guide them in a positive way. When a strategy is applied correctly, it helps shape the adolescent, then the adult, that your toddler will grow into and the decisions they will make later in life.

- Communication- One of the most important things about your relationship with your child is proper communication. Having an open channel of communication will let your toddler express him- or herself to you, without the fear of judgment. This leads to a better relationship in the future, hopefully one that will carry through your child's teenage years.

- Improved Behavior- All these factors lead to better behavior for your toddler. They learn to properly express their needs and emotions and poor behavior decreases as a result. You will no longer feel as stressed and your

toddler will
happier, or at lea
express and man
rough times.

Observing and Understanding Your Toddler's Behavior

Coming up with a discipline strategy for your toddler is not something that you can do or implement overnight. It takes patience and time because you are creating positive and healthy habits for your toddler. The very first step is to learn more about your toddler and how/why they behave. Follow these steps to observe and understand your child's behavior, so you can discipline them appropriately.

1. Observe Your Child as They Play, Sleep, and Eat- As a parent, you are always watching your child to some extent. Instead of looking for signs of trouble, however, spend your time watching them as they go about their day. Spend a couple days observing your child's behavior and looking for patterns that may indicate what areas need to be addressed. For example, you may notice that your toddler hides in the corner when he/she is frustrated. This would indicate that you need to talk to them more about managing frustration. While taking a 'time out' from the activity by hiding is a great sign of

a little self-control, you may need to address having your toddler share their feelings more.

2. Talk to Your Toddler- A critical part of proper discipline is having an open relationship with your toddler when it comes to communication. One of the biggest bad habits that parents get into is shaming their toddler for their behavior or showing too much disappointment. This discourages them and causes them to want to hide their emotions, which can cause serious emotional problems later. Instead, keep the channels of communication open. Rather than asking vague questions like "How was play time?" or "Did you

have fun at preschool today?", ask about what they built with their building blocks or how their art project went at preschool. Being specific will help your toddler communicate better.

3. Learn to be Empathetic- Spend a day thinking about what you would do if you were in your child's shoes. Try to label his or her emotions as they happen, by observing the situation and the behaviors that result. Consider what they may be thinking or feeling in that moment. Then, think about how you feel when you are experiencing the same emotion. By being compassionate to how your child feels, you will better be able to respond to their

needs and decide when discipline is needed.

4. Identify Problem Areas- As you observe your child, you are going to notice problem areas that must be addressed. Jot down the repetitive behavioral problems that you see. You will use this information later as you set boundaries and rules for your child. For example, you may use the three worst offenses as those that will put your toddler in time out.

5. Evaluate Your Toddler's Environment- Toddlers are sponges. Something else that you must consider as you think of a disciplinary plan is the role models that your child has in

their life. Do they have an older sibling or a caregiver with a bad habit they may be picking up on? For example, does your toddler's yelling when they are frustrated remind you of the way one of their parent acts when angry? It is important to remember how impressionable toddlers are— they are not the only ones responsible for the way that they behave.

6. Schedule Plenty of Quality Time- The economy today leaves many households with two working parents, meaning that children get to spend less time with the people who should care for them most. Even when work seems to get in the way, it is

important to schedule quality time with your toddler. Interacting with them one-on-one will boost your relationship and show them how much you care. It also fosters positive communication and gives you a better chance to observe your child and their emotions as they happen.

CHAPTER SUMMARY:

1. Toddlers are at a pivotal and stressful moment in their lives, as they experience a wider range of emotion and learn more about the world. To understand your toddler's behaviors, you must be aware of some of the most common reasons for poor

behavior choices. Toddlers often misbehave because they do not know how to express or manage emotions, lack self-control, are over stimulated, have a need that is not being met, want attention, or are just having a bad day. By narrowing down the problem, you can respond with an appropriate disciplinary action.

2. Before you begin using the advice in this book to discipline your toddler, you should sit down and come up with a toddler discipline strategy. This is important because it creates consistency, makes expectations known, improves self-control and decision-making, fosters communication with your

toddler, and improves behavior overall.

3. Before you can develop a strategy for disciplining your toddler, you must understand them and why they behave the way they do. Observing your child can be very helpful for this. Pay attention to how they behave playing, sleeping, and during meal times and encourage them to communicate with you. You can also learn more about appropriate disciplinary strategies by identifying problem areas, sympathizing with your child's emotions, considering their environment, and scheduling quality time with your toddler.

YOUR QUICK START ACTION STEP: CONSIDER YOUR CHILD'S BEHAVIOR

Right now, consider a behavioral habit that your toddler would like to stop. Research this behavior and a plan of discipline. This will give you practice on observing and understanding your toddler's behavior. Once you understand the reasoning behind what they are doing, you will be able to act more appropriately.

Chapter 3:
Effective
Communication:
How to Connect
with
your Child

Chapter 3: Effective Communication:
How to Connect with your Child

Effective communication and empathy go hand-in-hand when it comes to disciplining a toddler. When your toddler is struggling, they are going to look to you for guidance. It is important that you give them the chance to express themselves and learn how they are feeling. Then, you can respond with the proper discipline or redirection, to encourage better behavior in the future.

Toddler Discipline and Effective Communication

We have all been there. We have had a long day at home or a terrible day at work and the first thing we want to do when we get home is talk to a friend or our spouse. We express how the day made us feel and share what made us so upset. Toddlers, unfortunately, do not yet have the ability to describe the emotions that they are experiencing. This means that when your toddler cannot get his toy to turn on for the sixth time in a row and he chucks it across the room, it is only because he lacks the skills to communicate his frustration. Had he communicated, you may have helped your toddler figure out the toy—before it smashed into several pieces against the wall.

When it comes to toddler communication, effective communication means a few things. First, effective communication means that you have considered your toddler's behavior by considering how they are feeling at the time and how they might better be able to channel that emotion. Second, it means that you can speak about emotions and what your toddler is feeling with them. This 'labeling' is important because identifying what he or she is feeling will help your toddler express his or her feelings. Finally, effective communication means that you can help your toddler differentiate between good choices and poor choices. This involves helping your toddler learn the difference between right and wrong, as well as what is deemed acceptable and unacceptable by society.

Do not fret if you have not yet developed effective toddler communication for the purpose of giving appropriate discipline. This chapter will go into depth about how to foster positive communication with your toddler that will improve their behavior.

Benefits of Effective Communication

When you effectively communicate with your toddler for the purpose of creating a positive discipline strategy, there are several benefits, including:

- Improved Parent-Child Relationship- As children become adolescents, they tend to push their parents away and cut off communication. To help prevent this, it is important to nurture positive communication with your child as a toddler. By communicating effectively and without shaming them, you are teaching your toddler that they can come to you for anything— something that will be carried over into their adolescent years if you remain consistent.

- Increased Ability to Identify Emotions- When your toddler learns that they can come to you with problems, they will start to come to you when they are experiencing unpleasant emotions. It is important to always address these as being natural. Help your child redirect the emotion or let them talk to you about what is upsetting them.

- Better Problem-Solving Skills- Toddlers that communicate their emotions effectively have completed the first step to problem solving—identifying the problem. When your child comes to you with an emotional problem, talk them through it. By brainstorming what the child can do, you nurture their ability to solve problems on their own.

- Emotional Regulation- Parents who communicate effectively with their toddlers will find that their son/daughter can regulate their emotions better. This is a skill that will be very useful later in life as well, especially once your toddler must deal with the throes of adolescents in ten years.

- Teaches Empathy- When you communicate well with your toddler, they are learning that you care for them and how they are feeling. This models empathy, an important characteristic for your child to develop for healthy social relationships.

How to Establish Effective

Communication for Toddler Discipline

1. Take a Moment Before You React- When you react to suddenly, you do not give yourself time to be empathetic or come up with a plan for discipline. Unless your child is in danger, think about how they may be feeling or the reason behind their behavior. Once you have done this, you can approach the child.

2. Get Down on Your Toddler's Level- Do you remember how we discussed in the first chapter that yelling is not effective? This is especially true if you are across the room, away from your toddler. When your child is in

trouble, it is critical that you do not yell at them unless they are in immediate danger and you need to get their attention. Walk to the child and talk to them. Some children have trouble paying attention and they may stare in another direction or space off. To keep them focused, get down on their level. You can also place your hand gently on their shoulder or ask them to hold your hand while you talk to them.

3. Don't Demand Eye Contact- You should never demand eye contact when your toddler is being lectured. Even when you get on their level, they may hide their face because they feel ashamed. It is important that we

do not embarrass them further and make them look at us while they are being reprimanded. Keep in mind that your toddler does not have to be looking at you to be listening. Maintain your hold on their hand or shoulder and engage them in the conversation to be sure they are listening.

4. Talk it Out- To foster communication with your child, you should allow them to speak about what happened as well. Listen to your toddler and what he or she was thinking at the time of the incident. Encourage them to share their feelings and what they believe was happening non-judgmentally. This will let you gather information before you

decide what to do next.

5. Identify the Problem- Once your toddler has described the situation to you, help them identify the problem that got them in trouble. For example, if your child threw their toy, then you would explain that the feeling (anger or frustration) was not the problem—it was how they reacted to that feeling (by throwing the toy).

6. Find a Better Solution Together- Once your toddler understands what went wrong, you can help them think of a solution. Give them a chance to explain what they could do differently next time. If they cannot think of anything, guide

them in coming up with a better solution. Returning to the example of throwing the toy, the toddler could have asked for help instead or taken a break from the toy that was making him or her upset.

7. Discipline if Necessary- Once you understand the situation and have talked to your toddler, decide if further discipline is needed. For most first offenses, it is sometimes best to tell the toddler what will happen if the problem persists. The next time that they repeat the behavior, discipline them in an appropriate way and remind them what they should be doing instead.

CHAPTER SUMMARY:

1. Effective communication is a critical tool in toddler discipline. If you do not talk to your toddler and do not understand how they are feeling, you cannot give them the guidance they need to deal with their emotions. Without proper communication, your child may continue to have behavioral problems because they cannot form the relationships between consequences and their behaviors.

2. There are a number of benefits to effective communication when it comes to discipline, including a better parent-child relationship, the ability to label and regulate emotions, improved problem-

solving skills, and learned empathy.

3. It is never too late to start fostering healthy and effective communication with your toddler. By taking steps including thinking the situation through, getting down on your toddler's level, discussing the problem with them, and helping them problem solve before turning to discipline, you can encourage your child's development into a well-rounded adult.

YOUR QUICK START ACTION STEP: START COMMUNICATING WITH YOUR CHILD

Even though we have not gotten into the specific of discipline (that is coming in the next chapter), now is a good time to put the above communication strategy into practice. In addition to following through with this communication when your child misbehaves, be sure to engage with them when they are doing good as well. Encourage them to talk to you about their day and feelings regularly, to show that you are supportive and understanding of the emotions they may be dealing with. If you are especially busy or have trouble taking time out of your schedule to do this, set time aside in your schedule especially for communicating with your toddler. If you are not close to them, it may be the source of their bad behavior.

Chapter 4:
Discipline
Strategies

Chapter 4: Discipline Strategies

Troublesome toddler behavior can happen anywhere. However, there are some places and situations where toddler misbehavior is more common. In this chapter, we will focus on the most common places and situations when your toddler may need discipline to make the right behavioral choices. These strategies will be specific and helpful—as well as based on techniques that you can feel comfortable using without any stress or guilt.

Why You Need Specific Discipline Strategies

As mentioned before, consistency with your child is key to discipline success. By developing specific strategies, you ensure you remain consistent with consequences and the behaviors that you expect from your toddler. This is critical for toddler discipline success. Here are some benefits of using a variety of discipline strategies to encourage good behavior from your toddler:

- Consistency Among Caregivers- Many parents are not fortunate enough to be home with their toddler for most of the day. When there is more than one caregiver, a toddler can easily become confused about what is expected by each one. This causes misbehavior. When you have set strategies that you use for specific places and situations, all caregivers can refer to the guidelines as they discipline the toddler. This united approach will improve child behavior quicker.

- Lowered Stress Levels- Sometimes, a toddler's behavior can leave their parent wanting to pull their hair out. When you have a strategy for your child's behavioral problems, you can feel more in control in the situation. As an added benefit, your toddler will notice your collectedness and are more likely to accept that you are in charge.

- Targeted Approach to Discipline- Toddler discipline is not a one-size-fits-all approach. It is highly important that you consider your child's individuality as you choose the proper discipline based on the place or scenario. Some techniques will work better for some children than others. Even so, when you apply different techniques based on the specifics of the situation, you can find what works best and then implement it as part of your strategy.

Discipline Strategies for Places

In Public

When your child misbehaves in public, it quickly becomes a stressful situation for everyone involved. Some parents give into their toddlers in these moments, believing that it is best to get everyone's eyes off them as quickly as possible. If you do not want to encourage these behaviors, however, you must take the following steps:

1. Start by talking to your child about expectations beforehand. Any time that you take your child in public, you should set rules for expected behavior. If you take him or her to the park, for example, your rules may be that they cannot fight with other children and that when you say it is time to go, they cannot argue. In the grocery store, the rules may be that they are not allowed to wander away from their parent or touch anything. Set 2-3 rules and tell them what the consequences will be if they cannot follow them.

2. If your child does not listen, respond quickly by giving them

quiet time. This is usually done by keeping them near you. For example, you could find a bench to have them sit down on with you or you can have them stand between you and the cart while they are in quiet time. Then, allow them to go back to walking regularly once the time is up.

3. If they continue not to listen or they throw a fit over quiet time, remove your toddler from the area. Have them sit outside or away from the action with you for a few minutes and decide if it is okay for them to return once you have talked about the problem and what is expected of them.

At Bedtime

Bedtime behavior can be a struggle, especially if your toddler is over-tired or over stimulated from a long day. You should avoid punishments at bedtime because it creates negative emotions toward going to sleep that will cause more problems in the future.

1. One strategy that you should implement before your toddler goes to bed is to develop a routine. For my children, this involves each of them watching one episode of a show that they pick and then brushing teeth. We share a story and have bedtime cuddles, they get half a cup of water, and they go to sleep. Once you do develop a regular bedtime

routine with your toddler, be sure that any caregivers or babysitters are aware of your child's bedtime routine. Otherwise, your toddler may give them a hard time.

2. If there is something specific that you are struggling with at bedtime, sit down and discuss expectations with your child. Gentle guidance is best in this time because punishing your child when they are already tired will just yield negative results. Also, be empathetic toward your child during this time, as they may be having problems because they are overly tired.

3. If your child always asks for a small cup of water before bed, start getting it ready beforehand.

Some toddlers will postpone bedtime by asking for extra trips to the bathroom or more water. Have a pre-set schedule and make your child adhere to it every night. This consistency with rules will teach him/her what is expected at bedtime and they will give you fewer problems in the future.

Dinner Table/During Meal Time

If poor dinner table behavior is a problem, you will need to use a targeted approach. Addressing this problem at home is critical because the habits that your toddler learns at home will be carried over to daycare, school, family member's homes, and restaurants. Therefore, it is essential that you teach them not to throw food and to use good table manners.

Consequences can be useful for misbehavior during mealtime. Setting expectations is important as well. Here are some strategies you can use.

1. Start by establishing some dinnertime rules for at your home that everyone is required to follow. This includes things like using your silverware when you eat, sitting with the family while eating, or any other things that your toddler struggles with. Setting rules clarifies expectations for your child, so they are more likely to rise to the

occasion and do what you ask them to.

2. As you establish rules, you must also establish consequences. Decide how you are going to respond to your toddler when they misbehave at dinnertime, but keep in mind that you do not want to give them what they want. You can remove them and have them sit in quiet time until they are ready to behave or take them to time out if they will not be quiet. If throwing food is the problem, make your child pick up their mess. However, this may not be a good idea for toddlers who choose to throw their food because they want attention or because they do not want to eat

what they have been given. Regardless of the disciplinary action you choose for each of these scenarios, be consistent.

In the Car

Toddler behavior in the car can become distracting, which is a danger when you are trying to focus on driving. This makes quick action critical to prevent a stressful situation. There are a few techniques that you can use in the car, depending on what works with your child. This includes taking a privilege away from your child or creating another logical consequence. Another great choice is the 'energy drain' trick, which is described here.

1. Address the problem- For example, "I cannot focus on driving while you are fighting with your brother. It is draining my energy."

2. Follow with a Consequence- "If I do not have enough energy, I will not be able to play with you when we get home" or "I will not be able to take you to the park."

At Daycare

Daycares have a responsibility of caring for your children. They often use time out or remove kids from the situation, usually to talk to them about their feelings. If it is a serious enough issue, they will often talk to you when you pick your toddler up from daycare. In some cases, you may want to address the problem to reinforce the ideas that they learned after being disciplined by the daycare worker.

1. You should start by allowing your toddler the chance to tell you about what happened while they were at daycare. Remember to keep an open mind. It is okay to bring up the topic if they do not—but you should not do it in a way that can be perceived as threatening or punishing.

2. After the situation has been brought up, ask them to share how they were feeling at the time or what caused them to behave it. Then, come up with ways to solve the problem in the future.

3. Always remember that unless the behavior is severe, it does not require the idea to be drilled into your child's head or for them to be punished again. You can address it, but do so in a way that is conversational and encourages your child to share.

Discipline Strategies for Situations for a Child Who...

Hits

Your first reaction when your child hits you or someone else may be to hit them back. Unfortunately, when you hit your toddler, you are sending the message that hitting is okay and encouraging their aggressive behavior. Hitting is something where logical or natural consequences may not work as well. You need to remove your child from the situation and give them time to reflect.

1. Before you resort to time out, give your child the option of quiet time. Quiet time happens in the same area of the incident. Your child is not isolated. You sit with them while they are in quiet time for a set amount of time. Then, if they do well, you will talk to them about the problem (hitting) and that it means they are frustrated or angry. Help them come up with a solution to the problem.

2. If your child protests quiet time or will not sit quietly,

remove him or her to another room. This should be a designated spot in your home. However, to prevent negative associations, you should not make the time out area your child's bedroom.

3. Decide on the time that your child will be sitting in time out. Their time out does not start until they are quiet. As soon as it is up, spend time talking to your child about hitting, why they cannot do it, and better outlets for the emotions that your toddler was feeling at the time.

Screams

Redirection is a good tool when your child is screaming. This is especially true if they are screaming because of an encounter with another child or because they are frustrated. Rather than punishing them, redirect their attention to another activity.

1. Start by identifying the reason they are screaming and remove the object or remove them from the situation. Explain calmly that you are removing them or the object because they are angry/frustrated.

2. Next, get your toddler involved with something else. By saying, "Let's go get a cup of juice" or "Let's find a new toy to play with," you are giving your child the tool they need to walk away

and do something else when they are frustrated or angry. This will become critical as they learn emotional regulation and self-control.

3. If suggesting something to your toddler does not work, try giving them a task to do instead. For example, if they are screaming in the supermarket and redirection does not work, ask them to help you buy groceries. Let them pick the things they can reach off the shelves and put them in the basket. By keeping them engaged, you are encouraging helpfulness and keeping their mind focused, so they are less likely to have a meltdown.

Refuses to Eat

Refusing to eat is a common toddler behavior. Whether they 'don't' like it' or would rather be doing something else, it becomes problematic if your child is not getting the nutrition they need. However, note that not eating the foods you put in front of them is a common problem with toddlers. There are a few strategies that you can consider for this, but you should not really punish your child. You do not want to create negative emotions and pair them with eating.

1. If your child never eats dinner, then chances are, they will not want to eat most nights. Try putting something that they will eat on their plates if you are

worried about them being hungry. This could be a slice of bread served alongside whatever you are eating. If they continue to only eat the bread to fill their stomach, this can become a problem, so vary the things that you offer them.

2. Something else that you should do is make a big deal about the food and how good it tastes. Encourage your toddler to at least try the food—not even to eat it. Sometimes, getting them to put the food in their mouth and realize that it is tasty is the only missing step between a toddler that eats and one who does not.

3. If you know that your child does not like the food that they

are being served, meaning they have tried it and it does not suit their taste buds, ask your toddler about why they do not like it, so you can make food more suited to their taste buds in the future. If you are serving something for dinner they do not like, give them a few options that they can choose from. By creating choices, they have the option of choosing something they like to eat, but you remain in control.

4. Odds are, your toddler is not going to starve. Give them a multivitamin to make sure they are getting enough nutrition and speak to your toddler's doctor if you are worried. If you want to give them a snack before bed, be

sure it is unrelated to the dinner incident before.

5. If your child does not eat their food that they asked for, you can refuse to offer something else until they eat what was asked for. This is especially useful for daytime snacking, especially if your toddler tends to ask for things to eat and then smashes them or leaves them laying around. Explain the importance of not wasting food and put the snack on a table until your child is hungry enough to eat it.

Throws Things

Depending on what your child is throwing and if they are in danger because of it, you may want to let a natural consequence unfold. For example, if they throw they toy against the wall and it breaks, they have learned that if they throw their toys, they cannot play with them anymore. Alternatively, you can take the child's toy away as a form of logical consequence or place them in time out. To take away the toy, do the following.

1. Tell your child firmly to give you the toy. Explain that they threw it and now you are going to take it away and put it up for a designated amount of time. You can take away the toy for an hour or for a full day, but you should not stretch the punishment longer than this because your

toddler will no longer form the association between throwing the toy and losing it.

2. If your child will not give you the toy willingly, you should not give them the attention they are demanding by chasing them or taking it by force. If they will not give it to you, threaten them with quiet time or time out. Remind them that even if they give you a hard time, they will still lose the toy.

3. Once you have the toy, put it up where your child cannot reach it. If they did not give it up willingly, follow through with quiet time or time out.

CHAPTER SUMMARY:

1. You should not have to stress or feel guilty to discipline your toddler. The strategies discussed in this chapter will help you do just this—in any situation that may arise.

2. By coming up with a plan for discipline, you create the consistency that your toddler needs to form connections between the behavioral decision and the resulting consequence. You also shape your expectations, lower stress levels, create appropriate disciplinary plans, create a strategy that all caregivers can use effectively, and use a targeted and effective approach to disciplinary

situations.

3. There is more than one way to discipline a toddler in certain scenarios. By applying the techniques discussed in this chapter and the ideas for discipline provided in the first chapter, you can come up with a strategy that will be effective in getting your toddler to behave the way you want them to.

YOUR QUICK START ACTION STEP: CREATE A STRATEGY OUTLINE

There are many aspects of discipline that you will want to remember. In this step, outline some problem behaviors for your child and how you want to respond. This serves the purpose of keeping you consistent, especially since the disciplinary strategies applied are likely different from the ones you are currently using. Creating an outline and sharing it with other caregivers can also keep them consistent when it comes to appropriately disciplining your toddler.

Chapter 5:
Stressed Out?
How to Remain
Calm

Chapter 5: Stressed Out? How to Remain Calm

It can seem nearly impossible to keep your cool in the heat of the moment. Our natural reaction when children get loud is to get louder, by yelling or to get physical, by hitting. In these times, it is important to remember that the way that we react greatly impacts the behaviors that our toddler exhibits. Additionally, by reacting to the tantrum, we are giving the toddler the attention that they want—for all the wrong reasons.

It is natural that your child is

going to rebel, especially if the discipline strategies discussed here are not ones that you use already. As you try to communicate and discipline, expect your toddler to fight back. It is important to remember that this will not last forever and by staying calm, your toddler will learn that their bad behavior does not phase you—nor does it get them what they want.

Why You Need to Keep Your Cool

Imagine that you were standing in the office of the President and he is asking you for political advice. That would be absurd, right? You may lose confidence in him and question his ability to do his job if he is asking someone with limited knowledge about politics and international relations to give their advice on a situation.

When it comes to your child, you are the president. Your toddler looks to you as someone who will protect them from danger, catch them if they fall, and be there when they need help. If you yell or lose your composure, they are going to question your ability to lead. When you do stay cool, calm, and collected, however, you reap the following benefits:

- It Proves Your Credibility as a Leader- Your child

looks to you as the leader of the home. They will respect your authority, but only if they feel confident in your abilities to handle stressful situations. Being calm will show that you know what you are doing and your toddler will look to you when they are feeling unsure of their feelings or what is happening around them.

- You Can Focus on Effective Discipline- When you learn to keep your cool when disciplining your child, you can think much more clearly. This gives you the ability to implement strategies, rather than giving into the stress of the situation.

- Discipline Becomes Stress-Free- Becoming overwhelmed creates unnecessary stress that can leave you frazzled, exhausted, and wondering why after an encounter with your toddler. As you learn effective strategies for discipline, you will be able to handle problems without worrying about what you possibly can do to curb your toddler's behavior.

- You Will Not Feel Guilty After Disciplining Your Child- Sometimes, when parents lose their cool, they can feel guilty after an encounter with their toddler. This is especially true if they are too loud or spank the child because these are often ineffective methods that leave you questioning your skills as a parent.

- Home Becomes a Positive Environment Where Your Toddler Can Thrive- Toddlers respond well to calm, logical discipline. When you are calm, your child looks to you as support. You can guide them to make good behavioral choices and to handle their emotions in an appropriate manner. In this way, they are surrounded by the positive feelings and guidance that they need to thrive.

How to Use Positive Discipline When Your Child is Throwing a Tantrum

If your child is throwing a tantrum, the first thing you should do is assess the situation for danger. Consider if they are at risk for harming themselves and if not, let them throw the tantrum for a moment. Use this time to calm yourself, using deep breathing or counting. If you cannot relax over the sounds of your child's tantrum, walk away for a few moments.

Many times, once a child realizes that you simply are not responding to their tantrum, they will stop on their own. Once this happens, talk to them calmly about the situation and what emotions they were experiencing at the time. Then, help them problem solve as to what they could have done differently.

Often, temper tantrums result from a child not getting what they want. Be sure to explain that when your child acts that way, you cannot support their behavior by giving them what they want. Once they are doing the opposite behavior, be sure to provide positive reinforcement with your praise.

For example, imagine that one of your children has a toy and the other one tries to take it. When the second child is successful, the first throws a fit. When you take the toy away from the second child, they throw a tantrum.

With the second child, they should be removed to time out for taking the toy before you address the problem and how it can better be solved in the future. For example, you may walk them through scenarios where they ask the other child if they can share. Explain that if the child says no, they will not share, it is still not okay to take the toy. Instead, they should ask the other kid if they can have a turn once they have finished with the toy.

To handle the first child appropriately, you should return the toy that is taken. Before doing this, however, it is important to explain that throwing a tantrum does not solve problems. Instead, they should get an adult to handle the situation.

If you find yourself becoming overwhelmed, do not be afraid to walk away from the situation altogether. Be sure your child is safe first, then give yourself time to evaluate the situation. Think about how your toddler may be feeling and the cause of their behavior before reacting. This gives you time to logically consider the situation and respond appropriately, without yelling and without hitting.

CHAPTER SUMMARY:

1. Toddlers will naturally rebel as they start to learn the boundaries of the world around them. By keeping calm, you can implement a discipline strategy that comes without stress, without guilt, and with a high rate of effectiveness.

2. There are numerous benefits of staying calm when you are disciplining your toddler. Having a calm demeanor will make discipline stress- and guilt-free, as well as assure your child of your authority and create a positive environment where your

child can thrive.

3. It is okay, even encouraged, for you to walk away when you become overwhelmed with your toddler's behavior. By taking a deep breath or counting and giving yourself time to consider the situation, you make it more likely that you will choose an appropriate disciplinary solution. It is possible to deal with tantrums without hitting or yelling—you just have to have the clarity of mind to do it.

YOUR QUICK START ACTION STEP: USE ONE OF THE TIPS TO COOL YOURSELF IN TIMES OF

STRESS

The next time that your child is throwing a fit, use one of the strategies above to help yourself approach the situation calm and collected. Not only will you show your authority in the face of stress, you make it much more likely that your child will choose to listen to you.

Chapter 6:
Common
Mistakes and
How to Avoid
Them

Chapter 6: Common Mistakes and How to Avoid Them

In this chapter, we will discuss some of the most common mistakes that parents make when disciplining a toddler. It is very easy to make these mistakes—and the first step is identifying problem areas.

Common Mistakes When Disciplining a Toddler

1. Bribery- Bribery can be an effective method of getting your

toddler to do what you want—but only in that moment. There may be times when misbehaving is a lot more fun than the piece of candy you are offering for good behavior. Other times, your child just may not feel like listening to you. When you bribe, you also create an expectation that your toddler is only behaving to earn something. If you want them to behave consistently, it is important that you do not constantly give them gifts for good behavior.

2. Not Listening- As a parent, you want your child to give you their full attention when you discipline them. The problem is that some parents do not give their full

attention when their toddler is speaking. Remember that you must lead by example. If your toddler is communicating with you, turn off the television, do not pick up your phone, and give them the attention and respect that you want them to give you when they are being addressed.

3. Lack of Patience- Parents who try to implement disciplinary strategies may give up after a week, feeling like it is not working on their children. Something that you must remember, however, is that your child's behavior is not going to change overnight. Discipline is a constant process that is going to change with age. While your toddler's behavior will

eventually improve overall, it is critical that you put a full effort into the changes that you want to see. If you give up too soon, then the strategies will not have a chance to work.

4. Expecting Too Much- First-time parents especially do not have a good idea of what their children are capable of. Sometimes, we expect better behavior from our toddler, but do not take the time to understand what the root of the issue is. When you expect too much, you set your child up for failure. Instead, offer guidance in these situations so your child learns what you expect. For example, if you do not want them running

around the house on a nice day, consider taking them outside. They obviously need an outlet or a better way to redirect their energy. You cannot expect them to be still when they are full of energy.

5. Being Inconsistent- Inconsistency will confuse your toddler and make them unsure of what you expect. This leads to poor behavior later, as they push boundaries to try and define their independence and their place in the world. Additionally, inconsistency among caregivers can be a problem for the same reason. Your child may push boundaries with one person while behaving well for another.

Benefits of Identifying Mistakes

Before you can start correcting parent mistakes, you must know what you are doing wrong. It can be hard to look at our parenting style with a critical eye, especially when we are worried we have not been compassionate enough with our child. Keep in mind, however, that those are the mistakes of the past and by learning from them, you can start shaping a positive future for your toddler.

- Chance to Correct Them- It is never too late to adopt new parenting strategies and start guiding your child, rather than punishing them. Regardless of your child's age, you can implement new strategies now and with time, they will become the norm. The only way to know which of your discipline methods need replaced is to know which mistakes you are making.

- Reduced Guilt and Stress- When parents feel stressed or guilty after an encounter with their child, it is often caused by making a parenting mistake. By identifying mistakes and learning to avoid them, you can make a more positive experience for you and your toddler—one that you both feel better after.

- Better Relationship with Your Toddler- When you care enough about your toddler's well-being to identify and alter parenting mistakes, you are working toward improving your relationship. They will start to look at you as someone that should be respected for guidance, rather than feared out of authority.

How to Avoid Common Parenting Mistakes

1. Identifying the Mistakes- After reading through this chapter, you may already know a few things you are doing wrong. Remember that this is not a time to judge yourself—but to encourage learning and betterment. Becoming a better parent is something that will improve your life and the life of your toddler's, so it is well worth it.

2. Evaluate Your Emotions- How do you feel after disciplining your toddler? Do you feel confident that you have given them the foundation they need for emotional regulation and problem solving, or do you feel shameful or guilty about your tactics afterward? A little self-

doubt is okay, but if you are overly stressed or guilty about what transpired, you may want to evaluate your technique for mistakes.

3. Evaluate Your Child's Emotions- Your toddler will respond better when you use a positive parenting approach. If your child seems saddened or angry after your encounter, there may be some unresolved issues that need addressed.

4. Be Prepared to Accept Criticism- Sometimes, the biggest thing standing in the way when you try to implement a new parenting strategy is yourself. It can be hard to evaluate your own strategies, especially if you are

already doubting your abilities as a parent. Remember that the goal is to make a better life for your child. It does not matter what happened in the past—it matters what you do now.

CHAPTER SUMMARY:

1. The most common mistakes that parents make is using bribery to get their toddler to behave, not listening to their child, losing patience too quickly, expecting too much, and being inconsistent.

2. By identifying common mistakes that parents make when disciplining, you can evaluate your own strategies and make

adjustments where needed. This offers the benefits of giving you the chance to correct problems, reduced guilt and stress, and a better relationship with your toddler.

3. By making the necessary steps, you can ensure you are implementing better parenting strategies. You can do this by knowing the most common parenting mistakes, evaluating your emotions and the emotions of your toddler, and being prepared to accept criticism in a constructive way.

YOUR QUICK START ACTION STEP: IDENTIFY

COMMON PARENTING MISTAKES

For the next step, consider other areas of parenting that you feel stressed or guilty over. Then, do some research to find out if you are doing something wrong. By doing this, you give yourself the tools to better care for your toddler's disciplinary needs. As you evaluate what is wrong with your strategies, be sure to look up tips on how to correct these problem areas.

.

Chapter 7: How to Discipline a Special Needs Child

Chapter 7: How to Discipline a Special Needs Child

One of the emotions that parents often experience when they are raising a special needs child is stress. They constantly worry if what they are doing is right, even more so than the average parent. The good news is that what you have learned so far will provide a good basis for what you need to know to discipline a child with special needs and this chapter will teach you about the differences. It is possible to discipline your special needs child without guilt or stress—you just have to know how.

Benefits of Using a Unique Disciplinary Approach for Your Special Needs Child

Special needs children do not always have the ability to make the same associations in their mind as the average toddler. This does not mean that they are not intelligent. In fact, most special needs children are very smart— they just lack the connections needed to communicate well and respond to a regular disciplinary regimen. When you do find a method of discipline that works for your special needs child, you will experience the following benefits:

- Better Understanding of Your Child's Needs- As you teach your special needs toddler to understand their emotions, they will better be able to communicate their needs. In this instance, learning to listen to body language, not just words, is important. Be receptive to what your toddler is trying to communicate, even when they cannot find the right words.
- Improved Empathy- As you learn your child's special emotional needs,

your empathy towards them will improve. This alone can improve your parenting efforts because you understand them better. Researching your toddler's condition can be especially helpful in this regard.

- Improved Emotional Regulation- Like with disciplining the average toddler, choosing the right methods is going to help your special needs toddler regulate their emotions. This is incredibly beneficial since many of their social and learning disabilities come from an inability to understand

and manage their emotions.

Meeting the Special Needs of Your Child: Discipline for ADHD and Autism

Two of the most common mental illness that affect children are ADHD and Autism. This section will provide an example of gentle, but effective methods you can use.

ADHD

The major problem that children with ADHD have is that they cannot focus. Sometimes, they also make poor behavioral choices because they are overwhelmed by stimuli or bored with their environment. The key, therefore, is helping them learn to find the balance between these areas and focus in on what they should be doing at the time.

With children that have ADHD, you should expect to repeat yourself—even more than you would with the average toddler. Redirection is also an incredibly useful tool when children with ADHD become upset. By refocusing their energy and having them focus it elsewhere, it can eliminate problems.

Simplicity and routine are also incredibly beneficial for children with ADHD. Routines help your child learn what to expect, so they can focus at key points during the say. Simplicity is also important as you discuss rules and consequences—being too complex or using lengthy explanations will cause your child to misunderstand your or become distracted.

Finally, you will need to keep a close, watchful eye over your ADHD child. Their short attention span can cause them to misbehave or wander off if they become distracted by something.

Autism

One of the biggest obstacles you will need to overcome with your autistic child is communication. Rather than teaching them to communicate as you would, you must learn what types of communication work best for your autistic child. Use many methods of communication, including visual cues, gestures, written language, and verbal communication. You should also start with short, easy-to-understand sentences and slowly advance them.

Positivity is another big factor for autistic children. Be sure to state the behaviors that you want—rather than the ones that you do not want. Focusing on the positives will yield misbehavior. You should also constantly praise your child when they do something well, helping to form that connection between good behaviors and the good feeling that they get from praise.

Routines and schedules are also important for autistic children. This puts them at ease because they know what to expect throughout the day. This familiarity will encourage good behavior.

CHAPTER SUMMARY:

1. Special needs children require a slightly different style of parenting than most. It can be easy to become frustrated, but by developing a discipline strategy, you can improve the behavior of any toddler.

2. There are several benefits of choosing appropriate discipline methods for your special needs child. These include improved empathy, better communication, and a better understanding of your child's needs.

3. Two of the most common behavioral problems of children are ADHD and Autism. Both types of children benefit from a targeted approach that includes simplicity, routine, and proper discipline. You should also keep a watchful eye on your child and avoid physical punishment.

YOUR QUICK START ACTION STEP: LEARN

MORE ABOUT SPECIAL NEEDS DISCPLINE

One of the best things you can do for your special needs child is get educated. Instead of stressing, do some research to learn more about how to discipline your child. The techniques will vary slightly from what has been learned prior to this chapter, but as a whole, the positive parenting approach can be very beneficial.

BONUS Chapter: When Strategies don't seem to Work

BONUS Chapter: When Strategies don't seem to Work

While the ideal situation would be that every parent who read this book would implement the strategies and find success, there will be times when what you have learned just seems like it is not working. In these situations, it is important to keep your calm. Rather than hitting or yelling, try out the strategies in this chapter.

Why You Need to Tweak Disciplinary Approaches

While this book has been created

with the intention of helping parents become better disciplinarians, it is important to remember that there is no manual for parenting. Every child is unique and a strategy that works for one child may not work for another. Fortunately, with a little tweaking, you can easily change your disciplinary approach to reap the following benefits:

- Learning What Your Child Needs- The good news is that once you find a discipline strategy that works, it is likely to keep working. As you provide consistent methods, your toddler will learn to adapt to your needs.

- You Can Make Appropriate Adjustments- By analyzing your current methods and deciding what works and does not work, you can begin to make adjustments that work. This lets you discipline your child without feeling stressed or guilty.
- Your Toddler Will Behave Better- When you adjust based on your toddler's unique needs and personality, you will find a method that makes them behave. It is important to remember that yelling and

hitting are not good options—there are many other tactics out there to try when you become frustrated.

What to Do When Your Child...

Doesn't Respond to Discipline Efforts

If you are just starting to implement new discipline efforts, then it is going to take time before your child gets the gist of the situation. Remember to be patient—it can take several weeks of using a specific tactic before it is effective.

If your child still is not

responding to discipline efforts, try a new tactic. The first chapter provided you several methods to try. Give one that you have not attempted yet a chance and see if that helps curb your child's behavior. You can adapt it to fit your child's personality. For example, one child may respond better to taking away a privilege like riding their bike outside, while another may be encouraged to behave if you threaten to take away television.

Is Talking Back

Often, when your child talks back, it is because they do not feel they are being listened to. Instead of lashing out through yelling, take the time to have a conversation with your toddler. Consider their thoughts and feelings and give them a chance to explain. After listening to them, explain yourself and why you want them to do what you have asked. If they remain unreasonable, implement a consequence for their non-listening behavior and follow through with it.

Does Not Listen

If your child refuses to listen, then evaluate what is going on around them. If the environment is too busy, remove your child to another room or shut off stimuli like music or the television. Then, get down on your child's level and have them hold your hand or touch their shoulder gently.

As you talk to them, ask them to tell you what you said. Do not expect them to parrot this information back to you. Instead, have them speak with their own words and consider what they think you mean and what you really mean. If there is a difference between these ideas, then the problem may not be that your child is not listening—the problem may be miscommunication.

CHAPTER SUMMARY:

1. Disciplinary strategies sometimes need adjusted for you to successfully discipline your child. This is because each toddler is an individual and the

method that works for one may need to be adapted to work for another.

2. When you tweak disciplinary actions to fit the needs of your toddler, you will reap many benefits, including learning what your child needs for better behavior, making adjustments to achieve that, and experiencing better behavior from your toddler as a result.

3. By following a series of steps when your child does not respond to your effort, talks back, or chooses not to listen, you can develop consistency and expectations. Your child will eventually learn what is expected and what will result if they choose

not to listen.

YOUR QUICK START ACTION STEP: TROUBLESHOOT YOUR TODDLER'S PROBLEMS

If your child simply is not doing what you want them to, take the time to implement one of the strategies addressed above. It is important to remember that discipline takes time, but if a strategy is not working, a new approach can be beneficial. Always take the time to understand your toddler and be sure miscommunication is not the root of the problem.

Conclusion

Thank you again for owning this book!

I hope this book was able to help you to become a better toddler parent, by teaching you to raise your little one with proper discipline. It can be hard to sort through all the misinformation and advice that is out their regarding children, but by reading this book, you have taken the first critical step to getting toddler discipline right.

The next step is to put your strategy into action. You can start communicating effectively with your toddler for discipline today.

Through communication and observation, you can decide which strategies will be most effective. Then, tweak the strategies until you find something that works well for you and your child.

Finally, if this book has given you value and helped you in any way, then I'd like to ask you for a favor if you would be kind enough to leave a review for this book on Amazon? It'd be greatly appreciated!

Thank you and good luck!